COUNTDOWN TO SPACE

SALLY RIDE
A Space Biography

Barbara Kramer

Series Advisor:
John E. McLeaish
Chief, Public Information Office, retired,
NASA Johnson Space Center

Enslow Publishers, Inc.

40 Industrial Road   PO Box 38
Box 398   Aldershot
Berkeley Heights, NJ 07922 Hants GU12 6BP
USA   UK

http://www.enslow.com

Library of Congress Cataloging-in-Publication Data

Kramer, Barbara
    Sally Ride: a space biography / Barbara Kramer.
        p. cm. — (Countdown to space)
    Includes bibliographical references (p.) and index.
    Summary: A biography of the first woman in space, spanning her childhood,
career as an astronaut, and present life after NASA.
    ISBN 0-89490-975-4
    1. Ride, Sally—Juvenile literature. 2. Women astronauts—United States—
Biography—Juvenile literature. [1. Ride, Sally. 2. Astronauts. 3. Women—
Biography.] I. Title. II. Series.
TL789.85.R53K73   1998
629.45'092—dc21

[B]   97-21344
                                                                 CIP
                                                                  AC

Printed in the United States of America

10 9 8 7 6 5 4 3

Illustration Credits: National Aeronautics and Space Administration
(NASA), pp. 4, 7, 8, 10, 18, 19, 20, 21, 23, 26, 28, 30, 31, 34, 37; Smithsonian
Institution, p. 13; AP/Wide World Photos, p. 15.

Cover Illustration: National Aeronautics and Space Administration
(NASA) (foreground); Raghvendra Sahai and John Trauger (JPL), the
WFPC2 science team, NASA, and AURA/STSCI (background).

CONTENTS

Sally Ride, America's first woman in space, takes a break from her busy training schedule.

"Ride, Sally Ride"

June 18, 1983. It was almost dawn at the Kennedy Space Center in Cape Canaveral, Florida. The eastern skies were streaked with pink. On launchpad 39-A, astronaut Sally Ride was getting ready to climb into the *Challenger* space shuttle. In about two hours she would be rocketing into space.

Miles from the launchpad, crowds gathered. There had been a lot of interest in this flight. Much of it was because of Sally Ride. She was thirty-two years old and would be America's youngest astronaut in space. However, people seemed more interested in the fact that she would be America's first woman in space.

Two women from the Soviet Union had already orbited Earth—one in 1963 and the second in 1982. Now

Americans were excited about sending their first woman into space.

During the few months before, there had been many newspaper and magazine articles written about Ride. Television cameras captured her smiling face and her sparkling blue eyes. More than five hundred thousand people had traveled to Cape Canaveral to see the launch. Many of them wore T-shirts with the words *Ride, Sally Ride* printed across the front.

Ride was the flight engineer for this mission. During takeoff and landing, she would sit behind commander Robert Crippen and copilot Frederick "Rick" Hauck. Her job was to help them keep an eye on more than two thousand dials and blinking lights on *Challenger's* control panel. "There's an awful lot to watch up there, and we need a third pair of eyeballs," Crippen said.[1] Ride had a checklist of things to do if anything went wrong during the launch.

The other members of the crew were John Fabian and Norman Thagard. Fabian, like Ride, was a scientist. Together, they would run more than forty scientific experiments on board the shuttle. Fabian and Ride would also test a fifty-foot-long robotic arm.

The astronauts would ride inside a winged vehicle called an orbiter. It was one of three parts that made up the space shuttle.

The orbiter piggybacked a huge orange external fuel tank. It was the largest part of the shuttle—eighteen

Members of the Challenger *crew that blasted into space on June 18, 1983: (front center) Frederick H. Hauck; (back row, from left to right) Norman E. Thagard, Robert L. Crippen, Sally K. Ride, and John M. Fabian.*

stories high and twenty-eight feet wide. The external fuel tank was filled with liquid fuel for the orbiter's three main engines. The fuel from the external fuel tank would be used up during the lift-off sequence.

The third part of the space shuttle was the solid rocket boosters. Two of them were attached to the sides of the external fuel tank. They provided additional power for liftoff.

At about 7:32 A.M., the final countdown began.

"T minus thirty-five seconds. We're just a few

seconds away from switching command to the onboard computer," the flight director announced.

> T minus seventeen seconds and counting. The body flap and speedbrake are in launch position. T minus ten . . . nine . . . eight . . . seven . . . six. We go for main-engine start. We have main-engine start and ignition and liftoff. . . .[2]

Ride could feel the shuttle vibrate and hear the engines roar. Then the shuttle rose up off the launchpad in a cloud of smoke. The noise was so loud that Ride could barely hear the voices from launch control

Challenger rises off launchpad 39-A in a magnificent display of power, carrying America's first woman into space. The winged orbiter is attached to the large external fuel tank. Two solid rocket boosters are attached to either side of the external fuel tank.

through her communications headset. She forced herself to concentrate on the dials on the control panel.

Two minutes into the flight, the solid rocket boosters had used up all their fuel. They dropped back into the Atlantic Ocean. (They would be picked up and used again on future flights.) It was much quieter inside the orbiter now.

The spacecraft soared upward, powered by the orbiter's three main engines. Ride could feel great weight pushing against her chest and pinning her to her seat. This was due to increased g-forces, which were caused by the acceleration of the spacecraft. At one point they were three times greater than the force of Earth's gravity.

Eight and a half minutes into the flight, the external fuel tank was empty. It was jettisoned into space, where it would burn up before it could reach Earth. Ride was now experiencing the weightlessness of space.

Smaller engines on the orbiter were fired. They boosted *Challenger* into its orbiting position 184 miles from Earth.

The flight controllers at Shuttle Launch Control at the Kennedy Space Center had done their job. Communications with the crew were now switched over to Mission Control in Houston, Texas. Roy Bridges, an astronaut at Mission Control, asked about the flight so far.

The launch reminded Ride of trips she had taken to

Dr. Sally K. Ride, mission specialist, talks to the ground controllers from the flight deck of the space shuttle Challenger.

Disneyland as a child. At one time, visitors to the park bought "E" tickets if they wanted to get on the best, most exciting rides. Those tickets were not used anymore, but Ride thought about them now.

"Have you ever been to Disneyland?" she asked.

"Affirmative," Bridges answered.

"Well, this is definitely an 'E' ticket."[3]

Even as a child, Ride had been interested in the stars and planets. She had had a small telescope that she used for stargazing. However, as a child she had never imagined that, one day, she would be an astronaut zooming through space.[4]

Early Exploring

Sally Kristen Ride was the oldest of Dale and Joyce Ride's two children. She was born in Los Angeles, California, on May 26, 1951. Her sister, Karen, was born a couple of years later.

Sally grew up in the Los Angeles suburb of Encino, California. Her parents believed in letting their daughters discover their own interests. "We just let them develop normally," Dale Ride said. "We might have encouraged, but mostly we let them explore."[1]

Some of Sally's earliest exploring was in sports. She enjoyed street games of baseball and football with other children in her neighborhood. She was usually the only girl, but she was just as good as any of the boys. "When they chose up sides, Sally was always the first to be chosen," her sister recalled.[2] Sally dreamed of someday playing for her favorite baseball team, the Los Angeles Dodgers.

Dale Ride was a professor at Santa Monica Community College. He later became an administrator at the school. When Sally was nine, he took a year off from the college. The family spent that time traveling in Europe.

Joyce Ride had also been a teacher. While the family was in Europe, she and her husband tutored their daughters. However, Joyce Ride thought the trip itself was educational. "They learned as much traveling as they would have in school," she said.[3]

Perhaps she was right. When they got back to the United States, Sally was far ahead of her classmates. She was moved up to the next grade.

That was about the time she discovered tennis. When Sally was eleven, she began training with Alice Marble. Marble was a four-time national women's tennis champion. By the time she turned twelve, Sally was playing on the national junior tennis circuit. She spent her weekends competing in tennis tournaments across the country.

Sally got a tennis scholarship to attend Westlake School for Girls. It was a private Los Angeles high school. Some of her classmates were the children of famous actors and actresses.

Sally Ride spent her years in school perfecting skills that eventually helped her become an astronaut.

One of Sally's favorite subjects at Westlake was science. "I don't know what started me off on that track," she said. "There was no one person or one particular experience that I remember. My mom and dad didn't have any math or science interest."[4] She said she read a lot of science fiction as a child, but she read mysteries too.

Sally graduated from high school in 1968. That fall, she began classes at Swarthmore College in Philadelphia, Pennsylvania. At Swarthmore, she studied physics and played on the school's tennis team. However, Ride missed her family in California. She also wanted to explore another area: a career as a professional tennis player.

After three semesters at Swarthmore, Ride moved back to California. She took a couple of physics classes at the University of California at Los Angeles. She spent the rest of her time working on her tennis game.

For a few months, Ride practiced several hours a day.

It helped her realize that she did not want to be a tennis pro after all. "I wasn't that good," she later said.[5]

Her father disagreed. He said she was an excellent player. However, she did not meet the high standards she had set for herself. "She doesn't really compete with other people; her competition has always been inward," he explained.[6]

Ride began studying physics at Stanford University in Palo Alto, California. However, she thought she needed a break from all the science classes she was taking, so she also signed up for a class in Shakespeare.

Ride liked that class so much that she decided to take other literature courses. In fact, she took so many of them that when she graduated from Stanford in 1973, she had earned two degrees. She received a bachelor of science (B.S.) degree in physics and a bachelor of arts (B.A.) degree in English. She went on to earn a master of science degree (M.S.) in physics from Stanford in 1975.

Ride was finishing work on her Ph.D. degree in 1977 when she saw an announcement in the college newspaper. It said that the National Aeronautics and Space Administration (NASA) was looking for a new group of astronauts.

NASA still needed the experienced military and test pilots they had used in the past. However, the space shuttle was bigger than the spacecraft used by earlier astronauts. It meant that larger crews could travel into space. It opened the door for a new type of astronauts called mission specialists. These would be engineers, scientists, and physicians. They would not fly the shuttle. Their job would be to conduct experiments in space.

"Suddenly I knew that I wanted a chance to see the Earth and the stars from outer space," Ride later wrote.[7] She applied to be an astronaut the same day that she saw the notice in the college newspaper.

Sally Ride served as a research assistant in the physics department at Stanford University.

3

Getting on Board

More than eight thousand people answered NASA's ad, including over one thousand women. From those applications, NASA chose 208 finalists. The finalists were asked to come to the Johnson Space Center in Houston, Texas, for testing. Instead of having all the finalists in Houston at the same time, NASA divided them into smaller groups.

Ride was in a group of twenty finalists who flew in for testing in October 1977. First she was given a medical exam. She also listened to talks about what it was like to be an astronaut. After that, she was interviewed by two psychiatrists and by a ten-member selection committee. She spent about a week in Houston. Then she returned home to wait.

During the next few months, she finished work for her Ph.D. (doctorate degree) in physics. People who earn a Ph.D. are called doctors. When Ride received her degree in 1978, she became known as Dr. Sally K. Ride.

On January 16, 1978, Ride got a call from George Abbey. He was the director of flight operations at the Johnson Space Center. "We've got a job here for you, if you're still interested in taking it," he said.[1]

"Yes, sir," Ride replied.[2]

She was one of thirty-five picked for the astronaut class of 1978. They called themselves the Thirty-Five New Guys (TFNG), even though six of them were women. The TFNG began training at the Johnson Space Center in July. They were not astronauts yet. For the first year, they were called astronaut candidates (ASCANs).

During that first year, Ride spent most of her time in classrooms. She studied computer science and engineering. She also learned all about the space shuttle. Although she would not fly the shuttle, she needed to know how it worked.

She also spent about fifteen hours a week in the backseat of a T-38 training jet. It helped her learn about radio communications and navigation. It also helped her get used to higher levels of g-forces.

The plane had two sets of controls, one in front and one in back. The pilots sometimes let Ride fly the plane using the controls in back. She liked flying a lot. On her

Sally Ride walks away from a T-38 jet after another session of training.

own time, she took lessons to get her private pilot's license.

NASA had no special fitness program for the astronauts. It was up to each of them to keep in shape. Ride stayed fit by running four or five miles a day. Running was something she had started doing while she was in college. As an astronaut, she also began weight training. She joked that she needed to get stronger to lug around the forty-pound parachute she had to carry.

Learning to parachute was part of NASA's survival course. The survival course was the most physical part of Ride's training. She was dropped from a helicopter, four hundred feet into the water. She was left floating on a small raft in rough water. One time she was shoved out of a motorboat while she was wearing an open parachute. Then she had to get out of her parachute harness while she was being dragged through the water by the boat.

In 1979, Ride officially became an astronaut. It meant that she could now be assigned to a spaceflight. Each astronaut also worked on a special project for the shuttle. Ride was put on an engineering team. The team

Astronaut Sally Ride readies herself to leave the ground as she takes part in a parasail training exercise.

worked with a Canadian manufacturer to design the remote manipulator system (RMS).

The RMS was a fifty-foot-long robotic arm. It was to be used in moving payloads, or cargo, in and out of the shuttle's cargo bay.

The RMS was not easy to use. For the next two years, Ride spent much of her time learning how to operate it. When she found problems in the design, she suggested ways to fix them.

Ride also learned how to be a capcom. The word *capcom* is short for *capsule communicator*. It dates back to

At the Orbiter Processing Facility, the remote manipulator system (RMS) is installed in the cargo bay of Challenger.

Before Sally Ride entered space, she was the first woman capsule communicator (capcom). She spoke from Mission Control to the astronauts on the shuttle.

the early years of the space program when the spacecraft was called a capsule. The capcom is the only person who talks to the flight crew during a mission. Capcoms need to understand everything about the mission. They also have to be able to speak clearly and stay calm no matter what happens.

Ride was a capcom for the second and third shuttle flights. She was the first woman in that position.

In April 1982, NASA announced the names of the four crew members for the seventh shuttle mission.

They were: Robert Crippen, commander; Frederick "Rick" Hauck, copilot; and mission specialists John Fabian and Sally Ride. (The fifth member, Dr. Norman Thagard, was added in December.)

In July 1982, Ride married fellow astronaut Steven Hawley. It was the first time an astronaut had married another astronaut. It could have been a big news event. It did not turn out that way because Ride protected her privacy. She told only family members and a few close friends about their plans.

Ride flew herself to the wedding, which took place in Hawley's parents' home in Salina, Kansas. She wore blue jeans and a rugby shirt instead of a white wedding gown. The ceremony was performed by two ministers—Hawley's father, and Ride's sister, Karen.

Ride kept her maiden name. She would still be known as Dr. Sally K. Ride. She and Hawley settled into a three-bedroom home in Clear Lake City, Texas. It was near the Johnson Space Center.

After the wedding, Ride went right back to work. There was a lot to do to get ready for her first space mission. She studied the flight manual. It had step-by-step procedures for every part of the flight. Then she spent long hours in a simulator practicing each step over and over again.

A simulator is a vehicle that seems like the space shuttle in every detail except that it never leaves the ground. Computers are used to make it appear that the crew is in actual flight. Emergencies that can arise during the flight are programmed into the computer. In that way, the crew learns how to handle things that could go wrong during a mission.

Ride's training was often interrupted by reporters. As America's first woman in space, she had become a celebrity. It was not something she liked.

"It's too bad that society isn't to the point yet where the country could just send up a woman astronaut and nobody would think twice about it," she said.[3]

She did not want people to think she had been chosen for the mission because she was a woman. "I did

Some Challenger *crew members answer questions during a press conference; (from left to right) Robert Crippen, Frederick Hauck, Sally Ride, and John Fabian.*

not come to NASA to make history," she said. "It's important to me that people don't think I was picked for the flight because I am a woman and it's time for NASA to send one."[4]

Robert Crippen, commander of the flight, had picked Ride for this mission. He told reporters why he wanted her on his team. "I wanted people who knew the arm well," he said. "Sally and John [Fabian] were experts. I wanted a competent engineer who was cool under stress. Sally had demonstrated that talent. Sally also has a pleasing personality that will fit in with the group."[5]

Ride's husband, Steven Hawley, was scheduled to fly on the twelfth shuttle mission. Reporters asked him how he felt about the fact that his wife would fly in space before he did. "If they hadn't picked her, I think I would be mad, because I think she deserved it," he said.[6]

On June 18, 1983, Hawley was at the Kennedy Space Center. He was there to cheer on his wife as she made her first spaceflight. Ride's parents and her sister, Karen, were also there. They would watch the launch from a special visitor's area.

Seconds before liftoff, Hawley radioed Ride from Shuttle Launch Control. He had one final message. "Sally, have a ball!" he called.[7]

4

"You Should Have Been Up Here"

Ride said one of the best parts of space travel was weightlessness.[1] She enjoyed floating from place to place in the orbiter. It made no difference if she was upside down or right side up. Since there was no force of gravity, blood did not rush to her head when she was upside down.

She also liked the view. "You can see one thousand miles in any direction up there," she later said. "It's a perspective few people get. You get to see several countries at once, only you don't see any borders."[2]

It took *Challenger* ninety minutes to make one orbit around Earth. In one day, Ride would see the sun rise and set sixteen times. However, she did not have much time to enjoy the view. She had a lot of work to do, beginning that afternoon.

Ride and Fabian were scheduled to deploy, or release, a Canadian satellite during *Challenger*'s seventh orbit. This was part of NASA's plan to pay for some of the costs of exploring space. Flight crews could do work for other countries, private companies, and schools during the missions. NASA would then charge for these services. On this trip, the payload included two

This is how the northern part of Australia looked from the space shuttle.

cylinder-shaped satellites to be launched for other countries. The first was the Canadian satellite.

Ride and Fabian took their places at the control panel. It was located at the rear of the flight deck. There were windows that they could look through to see into the cargo bay. That was where the satellite was stored.

The first step was to open the sun shield. The sun shield protected the satellite from heat during the flight. Once the sun shield was opened, the satellite popped into position. It began to spin on a turntable. Then *Challenger*'s computer commanded the strong clamps holding the satellite to release. The 7,400-pound satellite floated into space.

The satellite had its own small rocket booster. Forty-five minutes later, when *Challenger* was a safe distance away, the rocket fired. It sent the satellite on its way to orbit over 22,000 miles from Earth.

Soon after the satellite was launched, Ride's first day in space came to an end. The capcom from Mission Control thanked the astronauts for a great day.

"You think it was a great day for you, you should have been up here," Ride said.[3]

The next day, Ride helped launch an Indonesian satellite. That country is located south of China in the Indian Ocean. It is made up of 13,677 islands. The satellite would make it easier for people on different islands to communicate with each other.

For the next two days, Ride was busy running

scientific experiments. There were more than forty on board. Some of them were for private companies and schools.

The highlight of the mission came on her fifth day in space. That was when Ride and Fabian used the RMS to launch a West German Shuttle Pallet Satellite (SPAS). The satellite looked like a flat cart, or pallet, piled high with packages. The packages were actually experiments.

Once again, Ride and Fabian took their places at the control panel. Ride called out the commands. Fabian pushed buttons on the control panel to lift the SPAS out

Challenger's remote manipulator arm grasps the Shuttle Pallet Satellite (SPAS). Sally Ride and John Fabian were the first astronauts to retrieve a satellite in space.

of the cargo bay. Once the SPAS was outside the ship, they let it drift.

The satellite appeared just to float beside the orbiter. Actually, both vehicles were speeding along at 17,000 miles per hour. Then Fabian snapped up the satellite with the RMS and pulled it back into the cargo area.

Next, it was Ride's turn to use the arm. Fabian called out the commands. The idea was to release and retrieve the satellite without using too much of the shuttle's fuel. "If you run out of gas in space, it is not a good day," Ride said.[4]

At one time, Crippen fired small engines on *Challenger* to move it away from the SPAS. A camera mounted on the satellite took photographs of the shuttle. They were the first photographs taken of the shuttle while it was flying in space.

All together, the astronauts released the satellite and retrieved it five times. Then the satellite was stowed away in the cargo bay. The whole operation took more than nine hours.

Ride and Fabian made a permanent change in space travel that day. They were the first astronauts to retrieve a satellite in space. In the future, scientists hoped to use the RMS to repair satellites in space and to build space stations. Ride and Fabian had just taken the first step toward making those dreams come true.

The crew had a lot of work to do during the flight, but they found time for fun too. Ride competed in a race

to see who could travel across the cabin the fastest. The astronauts used the cabin's walls to give themselves a push in the direction they wanted to go. Ride finished the race in second place. Fabian was first.

They also made up a game using a jar of jelly beans. President Ronald Reagan had given them to the crew as a gift. The astronauts released the jelly beans. The candy floated in the weightless conditions inside the orbiter. Then the crew traveled around the orbiter, snapping up jelly beans with their mouths.

The space shuttle had been launched on Saturday. On Thursday, their sixth day

This was one of the first photographs of Challenger *in space, taken by the SPAS satellite.*

in space, the crew began stowing equipment. It was time to get ready for their trip home on Friday. They were scheduled to land on a newly built three-mile landing strip at the Kennedy Space Center. They would be the first crew to use that landing strip.

Unfortunately, on Friday morning the weather report from Florida was gloomy. There were low clouds and light rain in the area. The orbiter had special tiles on the outside. They protected the orbiter from heat as it reentered Earth's atmosphere. The tiles could be damaged by the damp air. Taking time to replace the tiles could delay a future flight. NASA decided it would

Commander Robert Crippen safely lands Challenger *at Edwards Air Force Base, delivering Sally Ride to a group of cheering fans.*

be better if the shuttle landed at Edwards Air Force Base in California.

The change in plans was disappointing for NASA officials and for Ride's family, who were still in Florida. It was also disappointing for thousands of space fans who had gotten up before dawn to watch the landing in Florida.

People near Edwards Air Force Base had only four hours to get ready to welcome the astronauts. Because of the short notice, there was only a small crowd to greet them. However, they were a lively group. They cheered and waved posters that read, "Herstory made today by Sally Ride."[5]

At a press conference following the landing, Ride said, "The thing that I'll remember most about the flight is that it was fun. In fact, I'm sure it was the most fun that I will ever have in my life."[6]

It was not the end of her fun in space. A few months later, Ride began to prepare for another *Challenger* flight.

5

More Exploring

On October 5, 1984, Ride was back on the launchpad at the Kennedy Space Center. At dawn, *Challenger's* engines thundered. Then the spacecraft shot off the launchpad on a tail of flames.

There were seven astronauts on board. It was the largest crew to fly in space so far. Two of the crew members were women—Sally Ride and Kathryn Sullivan. Ride and Sullivan had been classmates in elementary school.

Ride was flight engineer for this mission, as she had been on her first flight. She was the first mission specialist to make a second shuttle flight. Sullivan would be the first American woman to walk in space.

On this mission, the astronauts would study Earth

from space. They would be using special radar equipment and cameras for that purpose.

The shuttle also carried one satellite. It would help scientists make better long-range weather forecasts. Ride was scheduled to deploy the satellite about eight hours after liftoff.

Unfortunately, the mission had a lot of technical problems. The first came that afternoon when it was time for Ride to deploy the satellite. The satellite had two solar panels. To save room in the cargo bay, the

The Earth Radiation Budget Satellite (ERBS) was deployed during Ride's second Challenger *trip. This satellite was to help with long-range weather forecasting. The white remote manipulator arm can be seen grasping the ERBS.*

panels had been folded closed. In space, they would be opened to catch the sun's rays. However, the panels would not open. The hinges were frozen.

Nothing like this had come up in flight simulations. Ride had to solve the problem using trial and error. What finally worked was to use the RMS to turn the satellite so that the hinges could be warmed by the sun. When they had thawed, Ride used the RMS to grab the satellite and shake it. The panels opened. She finally eased the satellite out of the cargo bay about three hours behind schedule.

On the second day of the flight, the astronauts ran into the opposite problem. They were trying to stow some radar equipment, but the radar panel would not close. Ride came to the rescue again with the RMS. She used it to reach into the cargo bay and close the panel.

"We got out the old favorite tool we've come to know and love so well," a NASA official told reporters.[1]

Other technical problems included a loss of communications. The crew was able to solve each problem and continue their work. At the end of the eight-day mission, the astronauts landed on the airstrip at the Kennedy Space Center.

Ride began preparing for her third mission, which was scheduled for July 1986. But on January 28, 1986, tragedy struck the space program.

A seven-member crew was to be launched that morning aboard the *Challenger* space shuttle. One of the crew members was Christa McAuliffe. She was a teacher, not an astronaut. She had been chosen to be America's first private citizen in space. Seventy-three seconds after liftoff, the shuttle exploded. All seven crew members were killed.

Ride was deeply affected by that tragedy. "Judith Resnik, Dick Scobee, Ronald McNair, Ellison Onizuka . . . We were all very close," she said. "Those were the astronauts I entered the program with."[2] Ride later noted that Judith Resnik had been sitting in the same seat Ride had used during liftoff on her own two flights.

Ride was assigned to a presidential commission to investigate the disaster. Their findings showed that the explosion was caused by faulty O-rings on one of the solid rocket boosters. After that investigation, Ride said she would never fly in space again because it was too dangerous.

Later that year, Ride co-authored a children's book with her friend Susan Okie. That book, titled *To Space & Back,* described what it was like to fly in space. Ride dedicated the book to the astronauts who died on the *Challenger.*

Ride later changed her mind about not flying in space again. She said that NASA had done a good job of redesigning the solid rocket boosters and making spaceflight safer. However, she would not have another chance to fly again soon. After the *Challenger* accident, there were no shuttle flights scheduled until June 1988.

Crewmembers of the space shuttle Challenger *that exploded on January 28, 1986: (front row, from left to right) Michael J. Smith, Francis R. Scobee, Ronald E. McNair; (back row) Ellison S. Onizuka, Sharon Christa McAuliffe, Gregory Jarvis, and Judith A. Resnik.*

However, NASA had another special assignment for Ride. She became the director of a NASA advisory panel. The panel was to develop a long-range plan for space travel in the future.

At that time, Ride was also thinking about her own future. In 1987, she and Hawley divorced. Ride never publicly discussed the reasons for that breakup.

A few months later, on May 26, 1987, Ride announced that she was leaving NASA. She had accepted a two-year appointment at Stanford University. She would be doing research at Stanford's Center for International Security and Arms Control.

Ride made that announcement on her thirty-sixth birthday. "The change is something I have been thinking about for quite a while," she said. "I've always wanted to come back to Stanford in some capacity."[3]

She stayed on at NASA until August. That was when she completed her study about goals for the country's future in space. That month she gave her report. One of the things she recommended was to establish a base on the Moon. There, as many as thirty scientists could live and work at one time. She also encouraged further study of Earth from outer space; using robots to explore space; and human exploration of the planet Mars.

In October, Ride began her work at Stanford University. She spent two years there. Then, in 1989, she accepted a position as a physics professor at the University of California, San Diego. She also took a part-time position as director of the California Space Institute, which is based in La Jolla, California. Her job at the institute is to coordinate space research among the University of California's eight campuses. She also works with California companies that are developing products for space travel.

Ride has written two children's books with co-author Tam O'Shaughnessy. The first book, *Voyager: An Adventure to the Edge of the Solar System,* was published in 1992. The second book, *The Third Planet: Exploring the Earth from Space,* was published two years later.

Ride is remembered in history as the first American

woman in space. Although she is no longer with NASA, she is still involved with space exploration as the director of the California Space Institute.

As a professor, Ride teaches college students who may one day travel into space. Through her writing, she has shared the excitement and the importance of space travel. She is a role model for girls who want to become astronauts and for anyone who dares to explore.

CHRONOLOGY

1951—Sally Kristen Ride born on May 26 in Los Angeles, California.

1968—Graduated from Westlake School for Girls in Los Angeles, California.

1973—Earned two degrees from Stanford University: a B.S. degree in physics and a B.A. degree in English.

1975—Received an M.S. degree in physics from Stanford University.

1978—Earned a Ph.D. in physics from Stanford University; selected to begin astronaut training.

1982—Married astronaut Steven Hawley.

1983—First shuttle mission, June 18–24.

1984—Second shuttle mission, October 5–13.

1986—Assigned to a presidential panel to investigate the *Challenger* accident; first book, *To Space & Back,* was published.

1987—Divorced from Steven Hawley; left NASA; accepted a two-year appointment at Stanford University.

1989—Resigned from Stanford; accepted a position as professor of physics at the University of California, San Diego; worked part-time as director of the California Space Institute.

1992—*Voyager: An Adventure to the Edge of the Solar System* was published.

1994—*The Third Planet: Exploring the Earth from Space* was published.

1997—Continues to teach physics at the University of California, San Diego, and to work part-time as director of the California Space Institute.

CHAPTER NOTES

Chapter 1

1. Sara Sanborn, "Sally Ride, Astronaut the World Is Watching," *Ms.*, Jan. 1983, p. 87.

2. Audio Highlights Tapes from NASA, "STS-07 *Challenger*," Lion Recording Services.

3. Ibid.

4. Ron Laytner and Donald Mclachlan, "Ride, Sally Ride: Her Place Is Space," *Chicago Tribune,* Apr. 24, 1983, Sec. 12, p. 1.

Chapter 2

1. Jerry Adler with Pamela Abramson, "Sally Ride: Ready for Liftoff," *Newsweek,* June 13, 1983, p. 45.

2. Michael Ryan, "A Ride in Space," *People Weekly,* June 20, 1983, p. 87.

3. Rogers Worthington, "Sally Ride's Down-to-earth Parents," *Chicago Tribune,* June 16, 1983.

4. Ron Laytner and Donald Mclachlan, "Ride, Sally Ride: Her Place Is Space," *Chicago Tribune,* Apr. 24, 1983, Sec. 12, p. 2.

5. Carol Hill, "Sally Ride: Hero for Our Time," *Vogue,* Jan. 1984, p. 90.

6. Mike Leary, "Countdown of a Pioneer," *Philadelphia Inquirer,* June 10, 1983.

7. Sally Ride and Susan Okie, *To Space & Back* (New York: Lothrop, Lee & Shepard Books, 1986), p. 9.

Chapter 3

1. Susan Okie, "NASA Appeal Gave a Physicist Wings," *Washington Post,* May 9, 1983, p. A8.

2. Ibid.

3. Frederic Golden, Sam Allis, and Jerry Hannifin, "Sally's Joy Ride into the Sky: The First American Woman to Fly in Space Shows She Has Got the Right Stuff," *Time,* June 13, 1983, p. 56.

4. Jerry Adler with Pamela Abramson, "Sally Ride: Ready for Liftoff," *Newsweek,* June 13, 1983, p. 36.

5. Michael Ryan, "A Ride in Space," *People Weekly,* June 20, 1983, p. 88.

6. Susan Okie, "At Home, Space Art and Trivia Tests," *Washington Post,* May 9, 1983, p. A8.

7. Mike Leary, "Sally K. Ride Is in Orbit," *Philadelphia Inquirer,* June 19, 1983.

Chapter 4

1. Sally Ride and Susan Okie, *To Space & Back* (New York: Lothrop, Lee & Shepard Books, 1986), p. 29.

2. Carol Hill, "Sally Ride: Hero for Our Time," *Vogue,* Jan. 1984, p. 89.

3. Audio Highlights Tapes from NASA, "STS-07 *Challenger,*" Lion Recording Services.

4. Sara Sanborn, "Sally Ride, Astronaut the World Is Watching," *Ms.*, Jan. 1983, p. 87.

5. Sharon Begley with John Carey, Daniel Shapiro, and Sonja Steptoe, "Challenger's Happy Landing," *Newsweek,* July 4, 1983, p. 68.

6. Ibid.

Chapter 5

1. William J. Broad, "Shuttle Moves Damaged Antenna to Face Satellite, Preserving Data," *New York Times,* Oct. 8, 1984, p. A16.

2. Michael Granberry, "Sally Ride in Academia," *San Jose Mercury News*, March 30, 1990.

3. Michael Harris, "Astronaut Sally Ride Accepts 2-Year Stanford Appointment," *San Francisco Chronicle*, May 27, 1987.

GLOSSARY

arms control—When a country limits or regulates its weapons.

body flap—The part of the orbiter that protects its engines during reentry into Earth's atmosphere.

capcom—The person who relays information from Mission Control to the flight crew during a space mission and who gets information from the astronauts in flight.

deploy—To move an object, such as a satellite, into position.

external fuel tank—A huge aluminum tank that is attached to the underside of the shuttle and filled with liquid hydrogen and oxygen to fuel the orbiter's three main engines during launch.

flight controllers—People at Shuttle Launch Control and at Mission Control who use computers to monitor the launch and flight of a space vehicle.

g-force—A force on a person or object caused by an increase in acceleration.

jettison—To discard an object to lighten the load of a vehicle.

Mission Control Center—A room filled with computers at the Johnson Space Center in Houston, Texas. From there, flight controllers monitor spaceflights.

payload—The cargo of the space shuttle.

O-rings—Large rubber rings used to seal the various parts of the solid rocket boosters.

orbiter—The main part of the space shuttle; the winged vehicle where the astronauts ride.

physics—The science of matter, energy, and motion.

remote manipulator system (RMS)—A robotic arm used to move cargo in and out of the space shuttle's cargo bay.

Shuttle Launch Control—A room at the Kennedy Space Center where the launch of a spacecraft is monitored.

simulator—A vehicle astronauts use to practice for their spaceflights. The simulator seems like the spacecraft in every detail except that it never leaves the ground. Computers are used to make it appear that the crew is in actual flight.

solar panels—Panels that collect energy from the sun.

solid rocket boosters—The two rockets attached to opposite sides of the external fuel tank. They provide additional power for liftoff.

space shuttle—The first reusable spacecraft. It is made up of three main parts: the external fuel tank, the orbiter, and the solid rocket boosters.

speedbrakes—Panels used to slow the orbiter on landing.

FURTHER READING

Cole, Michael D. *Challenger: America's Space Tragedy.* Springfield, N.J.: Enslow Publishers, Inc., 1995.

Hurwitz, Jane, and Sue Hurwitz. *Sally Ride: Shooting for the Stars.* New York: Fawcett Columbine, 1989.

O'Conner, Karen. *Sally Ride and the New Astronauts: Scientists in Space.* New York: Franklin Watts, 1983.

Ride, Sally, and Susan Okie. *To Space & Back.* New York: Lothrop, Lee & Shepard Books, 1986.

Ride, Sally, and Tam O'Shaughnessy. *The Third Planet: Exploring the Earth from Space.* New York: Crown Publishers, Inc., 1994.

————. *Voyager: An Adventure to the Edge of the Solar System.* New York: Crown Publishers, 1992.

INDEX